Pocket Guide to Occupied Japan

Monica Lynn Clements
and Patricia Rosser Clements

Schiffer Publishing Ltd ®

4880 Lower Valley Road, Atglen, PA 19310 USA

Designed by "Sue"
Type set in Benguiat Bk BT/Schneilder BT

ISBN: 0-7643-0728-2
Printed in China
1 2 3 4

Published by Schiffer Publishing Ltd.
4880 Lower Valley Road
Atglen, PA 19310
Phone: (610) 593-1777;
Fax: (610) 593-2002
E-mail: Schifferbk@aol.com

Please visit our web site catalog at
www.schifferbooks.com
or write for a free catalog.

This book may be purchased
from the publisher.
Please include $3.95 for shipping.

In Europe, Schiffer books are distributed
by
Bushwood Books
6 Marksbury Rd.
Kew Gardens
Surrey TW9 4JF England
Phone: 44 (0)181 392-8585; Fax: 44 (0)181
392-9876
E-mail: Bushwd@aol.com

Please try your bookstore first.

We are interested in hearing from authors
with book ideas on related subjects.

Dedication

We dedicate this book to the
collectors of Occupied Japan items.

Acknowledgments

Our thanks go to the contributors. A special thanks to Mary G. Moon and Angela Pilgreen. Also, we thank the people at Patterson's Camera Shop for all their hard work.

Contents

Introduction

Collectibles made during the American Occupation in Japan (1945-1952) encompass a wide spectrum. Paper goods, metal objects, porcelain and bisque figurines, cups and saucers, and china only make up a portion of what we know as Occupied Japan items.

As a result of the tireless work of the Japanese, Occupied Japan items exist in a myriad of styles. For example, the Blue Willow pattern, copied from the dishes made in England, was a popular seller. Staffordshire style items in china and figurines are popular with collectors, and pottery pieces such as dishes depicting thatched cottages resemble British designs. Crudely made ashtrays and vases depicting the Wedgwood style are also available. In addition, the Japanese emulated German produced lines. Figurines of children are similar to pieces made by Hummel. Porcelain figurines depicting couples or cherubs are numerous and are similar to the fine German designs, and the mugs modeled after the German stein are also common.

For the collector of Occupied Japan collectibles, an adventure awaits him or her. It is truly mind boggling to discover the variety of items exported to the United States from Japan beginning in the late 1940s. The political climate of the 1950s meant that these items were considered dime store merchandise, but these collectibles have now found a loyal following.

The purpose of this book is not to set firm prices but to serve as a guide.

Chapter One
History

The surrender of the Japanese on August 11, 1945, signaled the end of World War II. The agreement was finalized in a treaty signed by the Japanese on the battleship *Missouri* on September 3, 1945. General Douglas MacArthur remained in Japan to oversee such matters as the reestablishment of Japanese trade, and the rebuilding process was the beginning of the American Occupation of Japan. This period lasted until April 11, 1952. During this time, MacArthur worked to ensure that factories damaged by bombs were reconstructed so that goods could be produced and exported.

While production in Japan resumed, the products were not actually shipped to the United States until some time in 1948. Customs officials inspected the goods thoroughly to make sure each item was marked "Occupied Japan" or "Made in Occupied Japan." If items arrived in this country with no mark, a rubber stamp was used to add the mark. While some unmarked items did slip through without being noticed, they have less value without an Occupied Japan mark.

A varied selection of figurines awaits the collector of Occupied Japan items. The large porcelain pieces are the most valuable. For example, the horse and carriage pieces with several figures, a carriage, and a horse are in great demand. The tall figurines of men and women are striking and unique. These figurines have been chosen to be transformed into lamps. Other couple figurines have served as candle holders.

Carriage with man, woman, driver, and two horses, 5.75".
Courtesy of Angela Pilgreen. $195-225.

Another view of carriage, driver, and horses.

Left. Man wearing red jacket and blue and red pants, 15.25". $150-175.
Right. Woman wearing red and yellow dress with flowers, 15.5". $150-175.
The figurines are *Courtesy of Angela Pilgreen*.

Figurine depicting man playing violin, 9.25". *Courtesy of Angela Pilgreen*. $125-150.

Rear view of figurine depicting man playing violin.

Lamp with man and woman, 7". *Courtesy of Angela Pilgreen*. $95-125.

Left. Figurine depicting man playing violin, 9.25". $125-150.
Right. Figurine depicting woman playing musical instrument, 9". $125-150.
The figurines are *Courtesy of Angela Pilgreen.*

Candleholder with man wearing blue coat, 4". *Courtesy of Marcella Wagstaff.* $75-95.

Opposite page:
Lamp with man and woman,
11". *Courtesy of Marcella Wagstaff.* $65-75.

15

Couples as a single piece or in pairs as two separate figurines have represented a plentiful area of collecting. Often, designers chose to portray pairs with women wearing colorful dresses and men wearing tailcoats. Some figurines show the Colonial style couples in motion as if they are dancing. Other designers depicted the couples with the woman seated. In some cases, the man is shown playing an instrument. Finding the matching mate to an unattached figurine can be a challenge.

Left: Figurine depicting man and woman, 5.75". $55-65.
Center. Figurine depicting pair with man playing musical instrument, 5". $45-55.
Right. Figurine depicting pair with man presenting woman with rose, 6.5". $55-65.
Figurines are *Courtesy of Angela Pilgreen*.

Left. Woman holding fruit, 5".
Right. Man holding hat, 5". $75-95 for the pair.
The figurines are *Courtesy of Joyce Calhoun*.

The Japanese produced figurines depicting popular American and ethnic subjects. Types of figurines designed to appeal to American consumers were cowboys and Native Americans. Oriental figurines abounded as did depictions of Mexicans, blacks, Dutch, and Siamese figures.

Left. Bisque cowboy figurine, 6.5". $20-30.
Center. Bisque figurine depicting woman carrying basket. 5.75". $25-35.
Right. Bisque cowgirl figurine, 6.5". $20-30.
Figurines are *Courtesy of Angela Pilgreen.*

Left. Indian with hands clasped, 6.25". $40-50.
Right. Indian wearing blue and white feathers, 6.25". $40-50.
Figurines are *Courtesy of Angela Pilgreen.*

Children represent popular subjects. Hummel style pieces show the ability of the Japanese to emulate a popular art form made famous by the Germans. Along with portraying children with animals, a specialized type of figurine can also be found of a shelf item intended for the side of a fish bowl. For example, a variety of seated boys holding fishing poles proved popular.

Hummel style girl with basket, 4". *Courtesy of Joyce Calhoun.* $15-25.

Bisque collectibles represent popular items that are a challenge to find. The Japanese produced a variety of attractive pieces in bisque with cherubs. Figurines, animals, and wall hangings are just a few of the categories in which bisque was produced. These items were more expensive in the 1950s and often appeared in more exclusive gift shops rather than in dime stores.

Bisque vase depicting boy, 9.25".
Courtesy of Angela Pilgreen. $45-55.

Bisque planter with cherub, 5.25".
Courtesy of Mary G. Moon. $30-40.

Japanese factories produced vases in many styles and sizes. Once again, the Japanese worked to appeal to the taste of Americans by providing vases in the Wedgwood style of blue and white. Vases in traditional shapes abounded with floral motifs as did vases with figures of cherubs, women, children, and animals. The wheelbarrow, slipper, cart, or watering can shapes gained popularity. The colorful Satsuma style vase provided an alternative to the small vases with floral motifs.

Four Satsuma style vases, 2.5", and one vase in center with floral motif, 2.5". *Courtesy of Joyce Calhoun.* $15-25 each.

Animal planters continue to be popular with collectors. A common type of planter is the donkey pulling a wagon, and other animals such as cats and dogs are well represented. The Japanese exported colorful planters depicting birds and swans. Planters exist in several sizes and are a welcomed addition to any collection.

Animal figurines were numerous and inexpensive when they first appeared in dime stores and department stores for a price of mere pennies. Often, the animals depicted were given human qualities. For example, animals were shown playing instruments. Another example of the ongoing attempt by the Japanese to appeal to Americans' taste through imitating the English style can be seen in the Staffordshire style dog. Today, hard to find items include animals made of celluloid.

Wedgwood style ashtray, 2.5" x 2.5". *Courtesy of Michael R. Grove.* $12-15.

Celluloid deer, 3.5". *Courtesy of Marcella Wagstaff.* $15-20.

Left. Rabbit playing cello, 3". $9-12. *Right.* Rabbit playing drum, 3". $9-12. The rabbits are *Courtesy of Mark's Collectibles.*

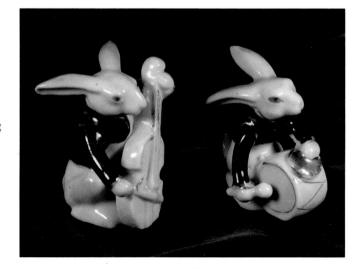

24

Staffordshire style dog, 7.75". *Courtesy of Angela Pilgreen.* $25-35.

Another category of inexpensive items produced in Occupied Japan is toys. The rubber squeaky toys remain more difficult to find. Windup toys have fared well and are much sought after because they have stood the test of time. Perhaps the most popular of the children's toys are the dolls. Dolls made of celluloid and bisque are common, and many of the dolls have movable arms and legs. A large selection of children's tea sets were exported to the United States, and these sets continue to be collectible although finding a set with all the pieces can present a challenge

Front. Watch, 7". $15-25.
Center front. Bisque doll, 3.75". $25-35.
Left. Dog figurine, 2". $12-15.
Right. Rabbit squeaky toy, 5". $25-35.
These items are *Courtesy of Angela Pilgreen*.

Opposite page:
Figurine depicting two cupids, 6".
Courtesy of Angela Pilgreen. $45-65.

Under the category of china, many items from decorator plates to cups and saucers can be found. Ashtrays with interesting patterns were produced as well as Wedgwood style jasparware pieces. Souvenir items existed that commemorated places or states, and decorative plates abounded. Tea sets have remained popular as well as whole sets of dishes. Complete sets have become prized by collectors. A Royal Beyruth style tea set in the red tomato style is available to collectors. The Blue Willow line has continued as a classic pattern that has pleased collectors. Noritake was the only factory not crippled by bombs during the war, so the company continued to produce dishes throughout the war. The company built a reputation for producing high quality dishes, and their Occupied Japan creations are distinctive and popular. The Japanese produced an unlimited variety of cups and saucers. Teacups and saucers have colorful handpainted designs. A large selection of demitasse cups and saucers exist.

Front. Silver metal hoop earrings with "Made In Occupied Japan" tags. $15-20.
Center. Piano, 2.25". $12-15.
Left. Pitcher with handpainted flowers, 3.25". $15-20.
Right. Leaf shaped ashtray, 4.5" x 3". $18-22.
The items are *Courtesy of Angela Pilgreen*.

Children's tea set. *Courtesy of Karen Reavis.* $35-45.

Front. Royal Beyreuth style individual creamer, 2".
Left. Royal Beyreuth style sugar, 3.25".
Center. Royal Beyreuth style teapot, 5.25".
Right. Royal Beyreuth style creamer, 2.75". $150-175 for the set.
The Royal Beyreuth style dishes are *Courtesy of Ruth Derbin.*

Blue Willow cup and saucer. *Courtesy of Angela Pilgreen*. $15-25.

Front. Saucer with floral motif. $12-15.
Center left. Saucer with pink roses. $10-15.
Center right. Saucer with gold colored border and flowers. $12-15.
Back. Blue Willow saucer. $12-15.
The saucers are *Courtesy of Angela Pilgreen*.

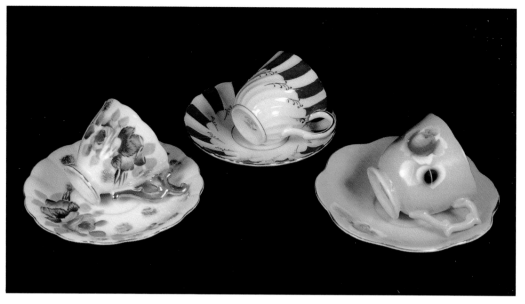

Three demitasse cups and saucers. *Courtesy of Angela Pilgreen.* $25-30 each.

Place setting with demitasse cup and saucer, butter plate, cup and saucer, bread plate, and dinner plate from Rosetti's Spring Violets pattern. *Courtesy of Joann Askew.* $75-95 for place setting.

Front left. Sugar bowl lid. $5-8.
Front center. Creamer. $15-25.
Front right. Butter plate. $10-15.
Back left. Vegetable bowl. $20-25.
Back right. Vegetable bowl. $20-25.
Rossetti's Spring Violets dishes are
Courtesy of Joann Askew.

Below:
Front left. Serving platter. $45-55.
Front right. Vegetable bowl. $35-45.
Back. Serving platter. $65-75.
The Noritake serving pieces are *Courtesy of
Jeannine Knight.*

Noritake china place setting. *Courtesy of Jeannine Knight.* $85-95 for place setting.

Front. Berry bowl. $12-18.
Back left and right. Soup bowls. $15-25 each.
The Noritake china bowls are *Courtesy of Jeannine Knight.*

Toby mugs caught the attention of collectors in the 1950s. These mugs are like other categories of Occupied Japan items. Some are more well made than others. They were produced to copy the work of artisans in other countries who designed similar mugs.

Left. Toby mug. $30-40. *Right*. Demitasse cup and saucer with floral motif. $30-35.

Toby mug. *Courtesy of Karen Reavis.* $25-35.

Left. Toby mug with man wearing gray jacket, 2.75". *Center*. Toby mug with man wearing red coat, 2.25". $25-35. *Right*. Toby mug with man wearing gray jacket, 2.75". $25-35. Toby mugs are *Courtesy of Angela Pilgreen*.

Profile view of Toby mugs.

Many items that fall into the category of paper goods have not stood the test of time. So the collector who comes across a paper item marked "Occupied Japan" knows he or she has got a find. Often, one thinks of fans or parasols when considering the paper goods category. Other colorful items do exist such as the colorful packets for needles.

Fan with floral motif, 7". *Courtesy of Marcella Wagstaff.* $18-22.

Needles and three colorful needle books. *Courtesy of Mary G. Moon.* $9-12 each.

Metal objects come in a variety of items. Musical instruments such as harmonicas are now sought after by collectors. Binoculars and opera glasses showcase the ability of the Japanese to produce glass as well as metal items. Ashtrays, salt and pepper shakers, trinket boxes, glasses, vases, dishes, and silverware are all items available to the collector who searches for metal ware.

A difficult collectible to find is glassware. Since the United States was proficient in the manufacture of glass items, the Japanese chose not to delve into this area of production. However, perfume bottles do exist that bear the Occupied Japan mark. Also, cobalt blue glass liners for metal items such as glasses or salt and pepper shakers were manufactured.

Cobalt blue glass perfume, 3". *Courtesy of Lyndy Raley*. $30-40.

Cobalt blue perfume bottle with clear stopper with bird. *Courtesy of Mary G. Moon*. $40-50.

The result of the production during the Occupation can be seen in the numerous collectibles bearing the Occupied Japan mark. While most collectors value the china, figurines, toys, vases, planters, and metal objects, lesser known collectibles strengthen anyone's collection of Occupied Japan items.

Opposite page:
Center front. Harmonica, 4". $18-22.
Center. Metal gun lighter. $15-25.
Left and right. Two metal goblets, 3.25". $15-20 each.
The items are *Courtesy of Angela Pilgreen*.

Chapter Two
Couples

Left. Man and woman, 4.5". $35-45.
Right. Man holding hat and woman with ruffles on skirt, 3.75". $30-40.
The figurines are *Courtesy of Mary G. Moon*.

Couple with man holding woman's hand, 5.75". *Courtesy of Karen Reavis*. $45-55.

Left. Couple with woman wearing red dress and man wearing white coat, 2.25". $20-30.
Center. Couple with man wearing green coat, 3". $25-35.
Right. Couple with man wearing hat and green coat, 2.25". $20-30.
The figurines are *Courtesy of Karen Reavis*.

Right:
Couple with woman wearing ruffled dress, 3.5". *Courtesy of Karen Reavis*. $30-40.

Left. Figurine depicting couple with woman wearing dress with flowers, 3.5". $35-45.
Right. Figurine depicting man with red coat and woman wearing dress with green, 4.25". $45-55.
Figurines are *Courtesy of Mark's Collectibles*.

Couple with woman holding man's hand, 6". *Courtesy of Joyce Calhoun.* $45-55.

Left. Couple with man standing and seated woman, 5.25". $45-55.
Right. Seated couple, 4.5". $40-50.
Figurines are *Courtesy of Angela Pilgreen.*

Left. Couple with man standing and wearing green coat, 3". $35-45.
Center left. Couple with harpsichord, 2.5". $40-50.
Center right. Man and woman dancing, 3.5". $40-50.
Right. Man and woman, 2.75". $35-45.
The figurines are *Courtesy of Angela Pilgreen.*

Left. Standing man and woman, 5.25". $45-55.
Right. "Souvenir of Niagara Falls" man and woman, 3". $40-50.
The figurines are *Courtesy of Marcella Wagstaff.*
Figurines are *Courtesy of Angela Pilgreen.*

Couple with seated man and woman with lute. *Courtesy of Sybil Pugh.* $45-55.

Chapter Three
Single Figurines

Left. Woman on motorcycle, 5.5".
Right. Man on motorcycle, 5.75". $150-175 for the pair.
The man and woman are *Courtesy of Mary G. Moon.*

Two couples,
each figurine
measures 4.25".
*Courtesy of
Mark's Col-
lectibles.*
$15-25 each.

Left. Man in yellow coat, 8.25".
$20-30.
Center left. Woman wearing pink
hat, 7.25". $25-35.
Center. Woman wearing hat and
carrying lute, 8.25". $25-35.
Center right. Woman playing
lute, 8.25". $35-45.
Right. Woman carrying basket,
8.25". $25-35.
Figurines are *Courtesy of Angela
Pilgreen*.

Below:
Left. Man wearing green jacket,
4.25". $15-25.
Center left. Woman wearing
dress with flowers, 4.25".
$15-25.
Center. Woman wearing hat and
dress with flowers, 5.25".
$25-35.
Center right. Man wearing blue
jacket and striped pants, 4.25".
$15-25.
Right. Man wearing dark hat
with plume and red jacket,
4.25". $15-25.
The figurines are *Courtesy of
Marcella Wagstaff.*

Below:
Left. Small Art Deco woman wearing dress with flowers, 3.25". $9-12.
Right. Art Deco woman wearing colorful dress, hat, and gloves, 5.25". $15-25.
The figurines are *Courtesy of Marcella Wagstaff.*

Below:
Left. Man wearing yellow hat and holding jugs, 3.5". $15-20.
Center left. Woman wearing red hat and carrying jugs, 3.35". $15-20.
Center right. Woman wearing dress with ruffled skirt, 3.5". $15-20.
Right. Man wearing blue coat, 3.5". $15-20.
The figurines are *Courtesy of Ruth Derbin.*

Left. Girl with flowers at feet, 6". $15-20.
Center. Woman wearing ruffled skirt with red apron, 7". $25-35.
Right. Art Deco style woman, 6". $15-20.
The figurines are *Courtesy of Ruth Derbin*.

Figurine/bell depicting lady, 4". *Courtesy of Angela Pilgreen*. $15-25.

Figurine depicting woman wearing dress with ruffles, 3.75". *Courtesy of Angela Pilgreen*. $25-35.

Below:
Left. Seated woman, 3.5". $15-25.
Center left. Man playing musical instrument, 4.5". $15-25.
Center right. Man wearing green coat, 5.25". $25-35.
Right. Seated man, 3.5" $20-30.
Figurines are *Courtesy of Angela Pilgreen*.

47

Left. Bisque girl holding dog and cat, 4.75". $15-25.
Right. Bisque figurine depicting woman with long blond hair. $15-25.
Figurines are *Courtesy of Michael R. Grove*.

Left. Woman wearing hat and dress with ruffled skirt, 2.75". $9-12.
Right. Woman wearing multicolored dress, 2". $9-12.
Figurines are *Courtesy of Angela Pilgreen*.

Left. Seated man playing instrument, 3.5". $15-25.
Right. Man seated in chair, 3". $20-25.
The figurines are Courtesy of *Mark's Collectibles*.

Left. Woman playing piano, 3". $40-50.
Right. Woman playing cello, 3.25". $25-35.
The musicians are *Courtesy of Marcella Wagstaff*.

Left. Woman and harpsichord. $40-50.
Right. Woman with violin. $20-30.
The musicians and harpsichord are *Courtesy of Karen Reavis.*

Left. Seated man playing woodwind instrument, 4". $15-25.
Right. Seated man playing stringed instrument. $25-35.
The figurines are *Courtesy of Ruth Derbin.*

Left. Delft style blue and white woman wearing plumed hat and carrying parasol, 5".
$35-45.
Center. Delft style blue and white man, 5". $35-45.
Right. Delft style blue and white woman carrying basket, 5.25". $35-45.
The figurines are *Courtesy of Karen Reavis*.

Left. Girl holding basket, 5". $20-25.
Center left. Religious woman, 6". $25-35.
Center right. Woman with flared skirt, 3.25". $18-22.
Right. Woman with blue skirt, 2". $10-15.
The figurines are *Courtesy of Karen Reavis*.

Left. Woman wearing plumed hat and carrying parasol, 5.25".
$35-45.
Right. Woman wearing three cornered hat and carrying
basket, 5.25". $35-45.
The figurines are *Courtesy of Karen Reavis*.

Angel, 4.25". *Courtesy of
Marcella Wagstaff*. $15-25.

Man in yellow
coat, 4.75".
*Courtesy of Ruth
Derbin*. $15-25.

Left. Man wearing red coat, 5.75". $20-25.
Center left. Man wearing red three cornered hat and green coat, 6". $25-35.
Center right. Man wearing blue shirt and holding hat, 5.75". $20-25.
Right. Man wearing blue coat and playing instrument, 5.25". $15-25.
The figurines are *Courtesy of Ruth Derbin.*

Left. Boy with goose. $12-15.
Center left. Boy with parrot. $15-25.
Center. Oriental boy. $25-35.
Center right. Boy playing instrument. $15-18.
Right. Boy playing accordion. $15-20.
The figurines are *Courtesy of Karen Reavis.*

Left. Woman wearing pink, yellow, and blue dress, 5.25". $25-35.
Center. Man wearing red coat, 5.75". $35-45.
Right. Seated man, 4.25". *Courtesy of Mark's Collectibles*. $15-25.

Man with green jacket, 3.25". *Courtesy of Marcella Wagstaff*. $12-15.

Bisque man playing horn, 4". *Courtesy of Ruth Derbin*. $25-35.

Ethnic Figures

Man pulling woman in rickshaw.
Courtesy of Marcella Wagstaff.
$45-55.

Woman with fan,
5.25". *Courtesy of
Mark's Antiques.*
$35-45.

Oriental woman, 7". *Courtesy of Mark's Collectibles.* $25-35.

Left. Man carrying jar on head, 5". $20-30.
Center. Man with hands on head, 5". $20-30.
Right. Dancer, 4.95". $20-30.
Figurines are *Courtesy of Angela Pilgreen*.

Man playing stringed instrument, 5.75".
Courtesy of Angela Pilgreen. $25-35.

Bisque figurine of woman wearing yellow dress, 6". $35-45.

Oriental man, 6". *Courtesy of Marcella Wagstaff.* $35-45.

Left. Oriental boy playing violin, 4.5". $20-25.
Right. Oriental boy playing instrument, 4.5". $20-25.
The figurines are *Courtesy of Ruth Derbin*.

Left. Oriental boy, 4.75". $15-25.
Right. Oriental girl, 4.5". $15-25.
The figurines are *Courtesy of Marcella Wagstaff.*

Left. Oriental man with bucket, 4.25". $15-25.
Center left. Oriental boy with green cap, yellow jacket, and blue pants, 4.5". $15-18.
Right. Oriental man with beard, 6.25". $45-55.
The figurines are *Courtesy of Ruth Derbin.*

Left and center left. Oriental man and woman, 4". $40-50 for the pair.
Center right. Seated Oriental man, 5.25". $25-35.
Right. Woman with colorful hat and fan, 5.75". $35-45.
The figurines are *Courtesy of Ruth Derbin.*

Left. Bisque Native American man, 6.5". $45-55.
Right. Bisque woman with fan, 5.5". $25-35.
The bisque figurines are *Courtesy of Ruth Derbin*.

Front left and right. Black figures playing instruments, 3.25".
$45-55 for the pair.
Left. Oriental woman, 4". $20-30.
Center. Mexican man, 5.5". $45-55.
Right. Native American man with dog, 3.75". $40-50.
Figurines are *Courtesy of Angela Pilgreen*.

Children

Left. Boy carrying basket of apples, 4". $35-45.
Right. Seated boy playing violin, 4". $35-45.
Figurines are *Courtesy of Angela Pilgreen*.

Left. Girl with basket of apples and goose, 2.5". $15-18.
Center left. Boy playing instrument, 2.5". $18-22.
Center. Seated cherub with instrument, 2". $15-25.
Center right. Girl with doll, 2.5". $20-30.
Right. Boy with watering can, 2.25". $20-30.
Figurines are *Courtesy of Angela Pilgreen*.

Girl with platter and dog, 6.25". *Courtesy of Angela Pilgreen*. $50-60.

Left and right. Figurines depicting girls with baskets, 2.75". $55-65 for the pair.
Center left and right. Figurines depicting girls with ruffled dresses, 2.75".
$40-50 for the pair.
The figurines are *Courtesy of Mark's Collectibles*.

Left. Woman wearing yellow shawl, 3.5". $15-20.
Center left. Girl carrying green basket, 3.25". $20-25.
Center right. Dutch girl, 3". $25-35.
Right. Dutch boy, 3". $25-35.
Figurines are *Courtesy of Angela Pilgreen*.

Above. Boy playing lute, 3.5".
$15-25.
Left. Boy with toy horse, 4.5".
$50-60.
The figurines are *Courtesy of
Marcella Wagstaff.*

Boy with trumpet, 4.25".
Courtesy of Mark's Collectibles.
$15-20.

Chapter Four
Planters and Vases

Bisque vase with roses and cherubs, 7.75". *Courtesy of Angela Pilgreen.* $175-195.

Bisque vase with flowers, cherub reading music, and cherub playing musical instrument, 5.75". *Courtesy of Angela Pilgreen*. $150-175.

Left. Bisque planter with girl and leaves, 5.25". $65-75.
Right. Bisque planter depicting flower and cherub, 3.75". $50-60.
The bisque planters are *Courtesy of Angela Pilgreen.*

Bisque planter depicting woman and shell, 6.25". *Courtesy of Angela Pilgreen.* $75-95.

Two pink vases with white roses, 4". *Courtesy of Angela Pilgreen*. $15-20 for the pair.

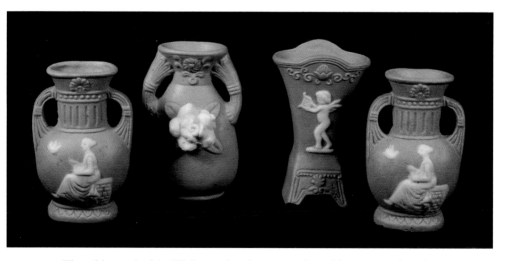

Three blue and white Wedgwood style vases and one blue vase with pink rose, vases range from 2.5" to 2.75". *Courtesy of Angela Pilgreen*. $15-18 each.

Left. Vase with rabbits, 2.25". $8-12.
Center. Vase with girl and blue bow, 2". $8-12.
Right. Vase with dogs, 2.25". $8-12.
The vases are *Courtesy of Angela Pilgreen.*

Left and right. White vases with pink flowers, 2.25". $9-12.
Center left. Brown vase with yellow and blue design, 3". $8-12.
Center right. Brown vase with blue, red, and yellow design, 3". $8-12.
The vases are *Courtesy of Mark's Collectibles.*

Left. Vase with floral motif, 3.5". $10-15.
Center. Vase with two handles and floral motif, 3.75". $15-20.
Right. Blue and white vase with floral motif, 3.5". $12-15.
The vases are *Courtesy of Mark's Collectibles*.

Left. Vase with flowers and leaves, 5.25". $12-18.
Right. Two handled vase with flowers, 4". $12-18.
The vases are *Courtesy of Angela Pilgreen*.

Left. Slipper vase with rose. $8-12.
Center. Slipper vase with pink floral motif. $8-12.
Right. Basket with blue flower. $12-15.
The vases are *Courtesy of Karen Reavis.*

Left. Yellow floral vase with pink roses, 3.5". $12-15.
Center left. White pitcher with red rose, 3". $8-10.
Center. Two handled vase with handpainted floral motif,
6.5". $15-25.
Center right. Vase with dog and basket, 2.25". $8-12.
Right. Satsuma style vase with Oriental woman design,
3.5". $15-18.
The vases are *Courtesy of Marcella Wagstaff.*
each.

Left. White vase with red flower, 4.25". $8-12.
Center. Orange and yellow vase with rose, 4.25". $8-12.
Right. White vase with yellow and blue flowers, 4.25". $10-12.
The vases are *Courtesy of Karen Reavis.*

Left. White vase with handpainted floral motif, 2.75". $9-12.
Center left and center right. Pair of slipper vases, 2.25" each. $15-18.
Right. Vase with pink rose, 3.25". $12-15.
The vases are *Courtesy of Marcella Wagstaff.*

Vase with Art Deco woman. *Courtesy of Karen Reavis*. $15-20.

Left. Vase with floral motif on wooden pedestal. $10-15.
Center left. Small vase with white flower. $5-8.
Center right. Tall two handled vase with floral motif. $15-20.
Right. Blue and white vase. $8-12.
The vases are *Courtesy of Karen Reavis*.

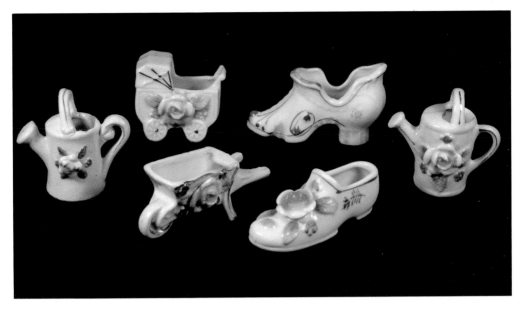

Small items ranging from 1.5" to 2". *Courtesy of Angela Pilgreen*. $12-15 each.

Flower vases ranging in measurement from 1.25" to 2.25". *Courtesy of Angela Pilgreen*. $8-12 each.

Front left, center, and right. Three planters ranging in measurement from 1" to 1.95".
$10-12 each.
Center. Elephant planter, 4.75". $12-15.
Vases are *Courtesy of Angela Pilgreen.*

A selection of six vases ranging from 2.5" to 4.5". *Courtesy of Angela Pilgreen.* $9-12 each.

Three Satsuma style vases ranging from 1.75" to 2.5". *Courtesy of Angela Pilgreen.* $12-18 each.

Pair of boot vases with floral motif. *Courtesy of Michael R. Grove.* $15-25 for the pair.

Left. Vase with man playing violin, 2.75". $12-15.
Right. Clock with floral motif, 2.75". $10-12.
The items are *Courtesy of Marcella Wagstaff.*

Left. Vase with dog and bow, 2.12". $8-12.
Center. Vase with pony, 2.38". $15-18.
Right. Vase with cat and bird, 3.12". $15-18.
The vases are *Courtesy of Karen Reavis*.

Left. Brown dog planter. $8-12.
Center. Bisque cupid vase. $15-20.
Right. Planter with white dog. $8-12.
The planters and vase are *Courtesy of Angela Pilgreen*.

Left and right. Animal planter with giraffe, 4.5". $9-12 each.
Center. Animal planter with owl, 2.5". $5-8.
The vases are *Courtesy of Marcella Wagstaff.*

Left. Pony planter, 3". $12-15.
Center. Dog match holder with handle, 2". $15-25.
Right. Duck planter, 3.25". $12-15.
The planters are *Courtesy of Angela Pilgreen.*

Left. Planter with donkey pulling wagon, 4" x 6.25". $15-18.
Right. Planter with giraffe, 4.25". $12-18.
The planters are *Courtesy of Ruth Derbin.*

Lamb planter, 4.5". *Courtesy of Mark's Collectibles.* $15-18.

Basket planter with dog, 2.25". *Courtesy of Marcella Wagstaff.* $8-12.

Left. Planter with cat wearing bow, 6.25". $18-22.
Right. Planter with cat and floral motif, 5.75". $18-22.
The cat planters are *Courtesy of Marcella Wagstaff.*

Left. Planter with donkey pulling cart. $12-18.
Right. Planter with pelican. $10-15.
The planters are *Courtesy of Marcella Wagstaff.*

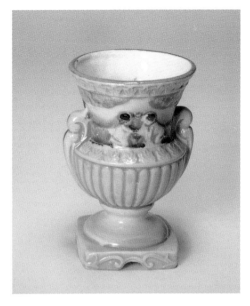

German style vase, 4". *Courtesy of Ruth Derbin*. $15-25.

Swan planter with red, green, and black feathers, 3.25". *Courtesy of Angela Pilgreen*. $15-25.

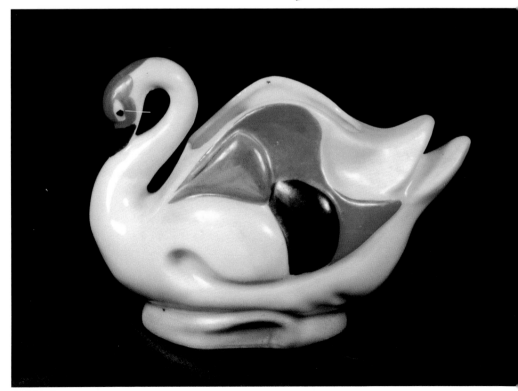

Swan planter with blue, pink, and yellow feathers, 5.25". *Courtesy of Angela Pilgreen*. $15-25.

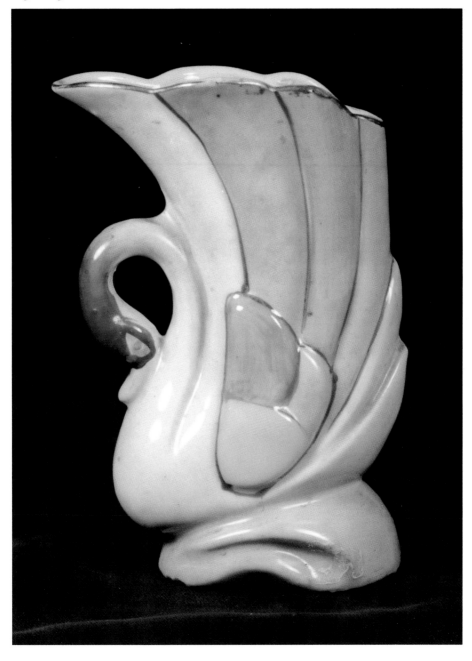

Parrot planter, 6". *Courtesy of Angela Pilgreen*. $30-40.

Chapter Five
Salt and Pepper Shakers

Left. Boy and girl salt and pepper shakers, 2.5". $35-45.
Right. Dutch girl and boy salt and pepper shakers, 2.25". $35-45.
Salt and pepper shakers are *Courtesy of Angela Pilgreen.*

Elephant salt and pepper shakers, 2.25".
Courtesy of Angela Pilgreen. $15-25.

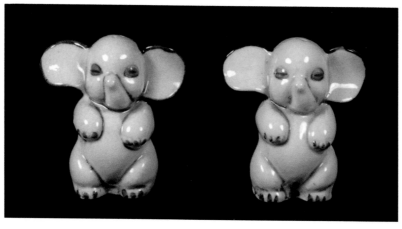

Left. Cup salt and pepper, 1.5". $15-20.
Right. Metal lamp salt and pepper, 2". $20-25.
Salt and pepper shakers are *Courtesy of Angela Pilgreen.*

Left and center left. Salt and pepper shakers in form of pitchers. $20-25.
Right. Beleek style shaker. $10-15.
The salt and peppers are *Courtesy of Marcella Wagstaff.*

Left and center left. Pair of salt and pepper shakers depicting Dutch girl and Dutch boy, 3". $40-50.
Center right. Shaker depicting girl, 3.75". $18-22.
Right. Shaker depicting boy playing musical instrument, 3". $18-22.
The salt and pepper shakers are *Courtesy of Marcella Wagstaff.*

Shaker of woman wearing red coat and blue skirt carrying yellow handbag. *Courtesy of Karen Reavis.* $15-18.

Salt and pepper depicting men with yellow hats, 3.25". *Courtesy of Mark's Collectibles.* $15-20.

Chapter Six
Animals

Chicken, 2.5" x 4".
Courtesy of Wanda Goodmon. $12-15.

Bisque chicken, 4.5".
Courtesy of Angela Pilgreen. $25-35.

Duck wall pocket, 6.5". *Courtesy of Angela Pilgreen.* $20-30.

Colorful figurine depicting peacock, 6.25". *Courtesy of Angela Pilgreen.* $20-30.

Parrot, 3.5". *Courtesy of Angela Pilgreen*. $20-25.

Left. Bird sitting on brown branch, 1.5". $10-12.
Center. Bird sitting on branch with flowers, 3". $12-16.
Right. Duck, 2.5". $9-12.
Figurines are *Courtesy of Angela Pilgreen*.

Left. Cat wearing blue bow, 2.25". $12-15.
Center. Cat with fiddle, 1.75". $9-12.
Right. Dog wearing red bow, 1.5". $12-16.
Cats and dog are *Courtesy of Angela Pilgreen*.

91

Left. Dog with clock, 1.75". $12-16.
Center. Dog and lamp, 1.75". $12-16.
Right. Dog wearing yellow bow, 1.5". $12-16.
Dogs are *Courtesy of Angela Pilgreen*.

Left. Dog wearing blue bandage, 2.25". $19-22.
Center. Smoking dog wearing green cap, 1.75". $20-22.
Right. Dog wearing blue bow, 2.25". $8-12.
Dogs are *Courtesy of Angela Pilgreen*.

Panda bear, 3".
*Courtesy of Ruth
Derbin*. $9-12.

Left. Figurine depicting dog and puppy, 2.5". $9-12.
Center. Donkey, 3.5". $12-16.
Right. Lamb, 2.35". $9-12.
The animals are *Courtesy of Marcella Wagstaff.*

Pair of ducks. $25-35 for the pair.

Laughing pig, 4.5". *Courtesy of Angela Pilgreen.* $19-22.

Chapter Seven
Toys

Peacock wind up toy. *Courtesy of Angela Pilgreen.* $75-95.

Miniature doll tea set cup and saucer. *Courtesy of Joyce Calhoun.* $15-20.

Bisque doll with movable arms, 2.75". *Courtesy of Karen Reavis*. $45-55.

An assortment of doll set dishes with cups measuring 1.5", saucers measuring 3" in diameter, and platters measuring 3". *Courtesy of Mark's Collectibles*. Cup and saucers are $15-20 each; platters are $10-15 each.

Front left. Doll's set creamer.
Front right. Doll's set sugar.
Back left and back right. Two doll's set saucers.
Back center. Doll's set cup and saucer. $50-60 for the set.
The doll's set dishes are *Courtesy of Ruth Derbin*.

An assortment of cups and saucers from doll sets, 1.5" to 2". *Courtesy of Angela Pilgreen*.
$15-20 for each cup and saucer set.

Left. Children's cup, 5.5". $10-15.
Right. Children's cup and saucer, 1". $15-20.
The children's cups and saucer are *Courtesy of Angela Pilgreen.*

Miniature tea set (lid missing from teapot). *Courtesy of Marcella Wagstaff.* $55-65.

Celluloid doll with movable arms and legs. *Courtesy of Marcella Wagstaff.* $35-45.

Chapter Eight
Dishes

Left:
Dish with peacock and flowers.
$15-18.

Below:
Left. Dessert dish with leaf motif, 5.25" x 5". $12-15.
Right. Dessert dish with handpainted scene, 6.5" x 5.5". $12-15.
The dessert dishes are *Courtesy of Ruth Derbin*.

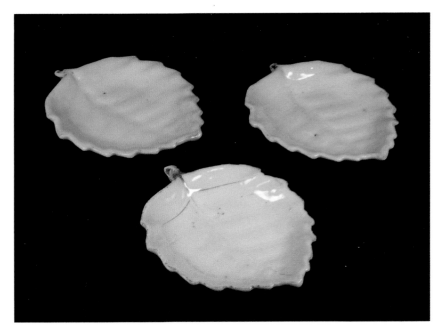

A trio of ashtrays, 3.75" x 3". *Courtesy of Angela Pilgreen*. $8-12 each.

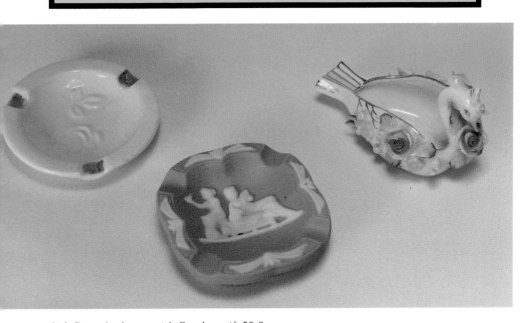

Left. Round ashtray with floral motif. $5-8.
Center. Wedgwood style ashtray. $12-15.
Right. Swan shaped dish with flowers. $12-16.
The items are *Courtesy of Karen Reavis*.

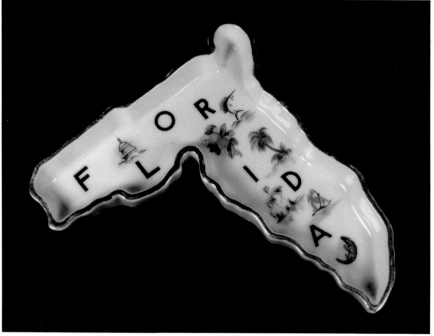

Florida dish, 5.5" x 4.5". *Courtesy of Angela Pilgreen.* $9-12.

Opposite page, top:
Front. Pair of ashtrays with floral motif, 3" in diameter. $12-16 for the pair.
Center left. Ashtray with pink rose, 3" x 3". $5-8.
Center. Ashtray in shape of a clover, 2.5" x 2.5". $8-12.
Center right. Ashtray with tulip motif, 3" x 3". $5-8.
Back left. Ashtray, 2.5" x 2.5". $5-8.
Back right. Ashtray with pink rose and leaves motif, 3.75" x 2.75". $7-9.
The ashtrays are *Courtesy of Ruth Derbin.*

Hira China dinner plate, 10" in diameter. *Courtesy of Marcella Wagstaff.* $15-20.

Gold Castle dinner plate with rose
motif, 10" in diameter. *Courtesy of
Marcella Wagstaff.* $15-25.

Gold Castle platter, 12" x 9".
Courtesy of Marcella Wagstaff. $35-45.

Spring Violets place setting. $95-125 for the place setting.
Front left. Bowl, 5.5" in diameter.
Front right. Cup and saucer.
Back left. Bread plate, 6" in diameter.
Back center. Dinner plate, 10" in diameter.
Back right. Dessert plate, 8" in diameter.
The Spring Violets place setting is *Courtesy of Ruth Derbin*.

Front. Gravy boat, 4" x 9.5". $15-25.
Center left. Vegetable bowl, 11" x 7.5". $20-30.
Center right. Bowl. $15-25.
Back. Platter, 14.5" x 10.5". $50-60.
The Spring Violets serving dishes are *Courtesy of Ruth Derbin*.

Left. Spring Violets sugar, 5". $30-40.
Right. Spring Violets creamer, 4". $25-35.
The Spring Violets sugar and creamer are *Courtesy of Ruth Derbin*.

Front. Soup tureen, 11" x 5". $45-55.
Back. Plate, 12" in diameter. $35-45.
The soup tureen and plate are *Courtesy of Ruth Derbin*.

Left. Spring Violets three tiered serving piece, 15". $45-55.
Right. Spring Violets two tiered serving dish, 12". $35-45.
The serving pieces are *Courtesy of Ruth Derbin*.

Left. Plate with scene. $35-45.
Right. Plate with scene of water and cottage. $35-45.
The plates are *Courtesy of Karen Reavis*.

Spring Violets handpainted plate with handle, 5.75" in diameter. *Courtesy of Joann Askew.* $20-25.

Left and right. Plates with one handle, 6" in diameter. $12-15.
Center. Plate with handpainted flowers, 5" in diameter. $12-15.
Back center. Souvenir plate from Greenville, Mississippi, in plate holder with blue and yellow flowers and multicolored border, 6.25" in diameter. $9-12.
The plates are *Courtesy of Angela Pilgreen.*

Left. Handpainted plate with fruit scene, 6" in diameter. $15-18.
Right. Handpainted plate with colorful flowers, 6.5" in diameter. $18-22.
The plates are *Courtesy of Angela Pilgreen.*

Souvenir plate of Greenville, Mississippi, with blue and yellow flowers and multicolored border, 6.25" in diameter. *Courtesy of Angela Pilgreen.* $9-12.

Left. Plate with four bouquets of flowers. $15-18.
Center. White plate with pink flowers at center. $15-18.
Right. Plate with roses and gold trim. $9-12.
The plates are *Courtesy of Karen Reavis.*

Left. Nut dish with figure of woman, 4.25". $20-30.
Right. Dish, 8.5" x 1.5". $18-22.
The dishes are *Courtesy of Angela Pilgreen.*

Left. Cup and saucer. $25-28.
Right. Butter dish. $10-15.
The items are *Courtesy of Karen Reavis.*

Opposite page, bottom:
Refreshment dish and cup in blue with floral motif. *Courtesy of Ruth Derbin.* $16-18.

Front left. Saucer with red flower, 4.25" in diameter. $10-12.
Front right. Saucer with two flowers, 4.25" in diameter. $10-12.
Back left. Saucer with bouquet of flowers on each side, 6.25" in diameter. $14-16.
Back right. Saucer with three bouquets of flowers, 5.5". $16-18.
The saucers are *Courtesy of Ruth Derbin.*

Trio of cups and saucers (from set of 6). *Courtesy of Ruth Derbin.*

Trio of flowered bowls, 5.5" in diameter. *Courtesy of Ruth Derbin.* $18-22 each.

Left. Cup with floral motif, 1.25". $18-22.
Center. Teapot with floral motif, 4.75". $30-40.
Right. Creamer with floral motif, 2". $20-22.
The cup, teapot, and creamer are *Courtesy of Ruth Derbin*.

Dish with floral motif, 7" in diameter. *Courtesy of Ruth Derbin*. $18-22.

Plate with handpainted scene, 8" in diameter. *Courtesy of Michael R. Grove.* $22-26.

Brown platter, 7" x 7". *Courtesy of Marcella Wagstaff.* $25-35.

Iris handcrafted plate, 10" in diameter. *Courtesy of Marcella Wagstaff.* $25-35.

Front. Pair of cups and saucers.
Center left. Sugar, 3.25".
Center. Teapot, 6.5".
Center right. Creamer, 3.25". $65-75 for the set.
The dishes are *Courtesy of Angela Pilgreen.*

Teapot, 3.25". *Courtesy of Marcella Wagstaff.* $25-35.

Cup and saucer with green and gold stripes. *Courtesy of Jennie's Antique Mall, Texarkana, Texas.* $26-28.

Another view of cup and saucer to show mark on bottom of cup.

Left. Cup with scene and saucer, 2.5". $19-22.
Right. Cup and saucer with floral motif, 3". $26-28.
The cups and saucers are *Courtesy of Marcella Wagstaff.*

Blue Willow cup and saucer. *Courtesy of Mary G. Moon*. $25-30.

Another view of Blue Willow saucer to show mark.

Another view of cup to show mark.

Pair of cups with floral motif (cup on left is
turned to show reverse design). *Courtesy of Angela
Pilgreen.* $22-26 each.

Left. Cup with floral motif and blue border. $12-14.
Right. Small cup with floral motif. $14-16.
The cups are *Courtesy of Marcella Wagstaff*.

Front left. Demitasse cup and saucer with cherry motif, 2.5". $25-35.
Front right. Demitasse cup and saucer in Dragonware design, 2". $25-35.
Back left. Demitasse cup and saucer with gold design, 3.5". $25-35.
Back right. Demitasse cup and saucer with chintz design, 3". $25-35.
The demitasse cups and saucers are *Courtesy of Angela Pilgreen.*

Front left. Demitasse cup and saucer with royal blue and floral design, 3.25". $25-35.
Front right. Demitasse in red and white with floral design, 3". $25-35.
Back left and right. Cup and saucer with yellow flower, 2.5". $25-35.
The demitasse cups and saucers are *Courtesy of Angela Pilgreen*.

Three cups and saucers. *Courtesy of Angela Pilgreen.* $30-35 each.

Three different cups and saucers. *Courtesy of Angela Pilgreen*. $30-35.

Demitasse cups and saucers. *Courtesy of Angela Pilgreen*. $25-35 each.

Four demitasse cups and saucers. *Courtesy of Angela Pilgreen*. $25-35 each.

Left. White pitcher with Chimney Rock, North Carolina, design, 2.75". $9-12.
Right. Yellow pitcher with floral motif, 3". $9-12.
The pitchers are *Courtesy of Marcella Wagstaff*.

Left and right. Small bowls with floral motif and blue and white scenes on outside, each 2" in diameter. $12-18 each.
Center. Blue and white bowl with floral motif, 3" in diameter. $22-26.
The bowls are *Courtesy of Marcella Wagstaff.*

Front. Dish with floral motif, 5" x 3.5". $18-22.
Back left and right. Ashtrays with apple motif. $9-12 each.
The dishes are *Courtesy of Marcella Wagstaff.*

Chapter Nine
Mugs

Mug in shape of barrel with steer and figure of man on handle, 5". *Courtesy of Angela Pilgreen.* $25-35.

Another view of mug to show steer.

German stein style mug, with blue and white design, 6.5". *Courtesy of Ruth Derbin.* $25-35.

German stein style mug with colorful scene. *Courtesy of Tim Greathouse.* $30-40.

Left. Mug depicting horse and carriage, 4". $20-25.
Right. Elephant mug, 5". $25-30.
The mugs are *Courtesy of Angela Pilgreen.*

Left. Mug with red grapes and grape leaves, 4". $20-25.
Right. Mug with purple grapes, 4". $20-25.
The mugs are *Courtesy of Angela Pilgreen.*

Chapter Ten

Wall Plaques

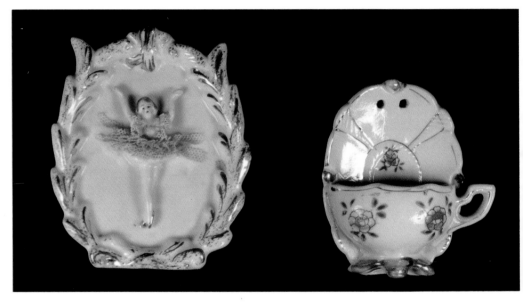

Left. Wall plaque with ballerina, 4" x 3.25".
$15-25.
Right. Cup and saucer wall plaque, 3.25"
x 2.25". $15-25.
The wall plaques are *Courtesy of Angela
Pilgreen*.

Cup and saucer wall plaque. *Courtesy
of Joyce Calhoun*. $15-25.

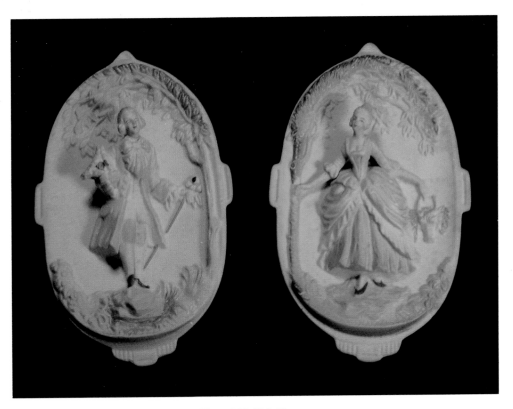

Left. Bisque man wall plaque, 7.25" x 4.25". $35-45.
Right. Bisque woman wall plaque, 7.25" x 4.25". $35-45.
The bisque wall plaques are *Courtesy of Angela Pilgreen.*

Plaque with pink flowers, 5.5" x 6.5". *Courtesy of Angela Pilgreen.* $25-35.

Chapter Eleven
Metal Objects

Binoculars, 7.25". *Courtesy of Angela Pilgreen.* $75-95.

Metal tray. *Courtesy of Karen Reavis.* $12-15.

Left. Piano trinket box, 2". $15-20.
Center left. Metal handwarmer, 4" x 2.75". $15-20.
Center. Tea infuser, 1.25". $10-15.
Center right. Metal set, 1.25". $15-25.
Center back. Ashtray, 5" x 6.25". $15-20.
The metal items are *Courtesy of Angela Pilgreen.*

Metal tray with six metal glasses, tray is 5.5" x 10.5", and glasses are 4". *Courtesy of Marcella Wagstaff.* $55-65.

Silver metal vase with floral motif, 7" x 5". *Courtesy of Wanda Goodmon.* $25-35.

Metal cigarette lighter in shape of gun. *Courtesy of Wanda Goodmon.* $15-25.

74-piece silverware set, marked SEKI K.K.K. EPNS. *Courtesy of Angela Pilgreen.* $295-325.

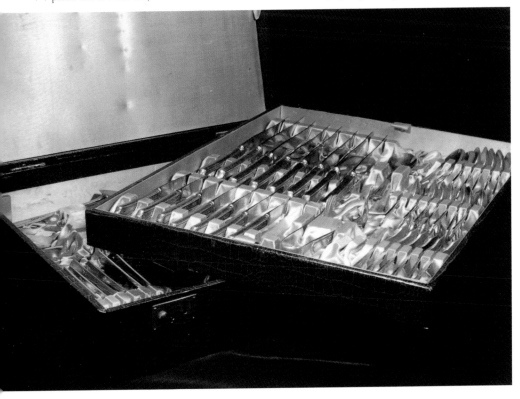

Gift set containing metal tray, salt, pepper, and jam jar with cobalt blue glass linings, and spoon. *Courtesy of Angela Pilgreen.* $55-65.

Left. Metal tea infuser. $9-12.
Right. Metal tea infuser. $12-16.
The metal items are *Courtesy of Tim Greathouse.*

Metal piano trinket box. *Courtesy of Marcella Wagstaff.* $15-20.

Chapter Twelve

Miscellaneous Objects

Enlarged view of identification tag
on sewing machine.

Tru-Sew sewing machine. *Courtesy of
Mary G. Moon*. $150-175.

Left. Metal opera glasses. $95-125.
Center. Tray, 5". $18-22.
Center right. Perfume bottle, 2.5". $15-20.
Right. Trinket box, 3.5".
The items are *Courtesy of Angela Pilgreen.*

Trinket box. *Courtesy of Kenneth L. Surratt, Jr.* $9-12.

Clock with case "Made in Occupied Japan" and clock "Made in the U.S.," 7.75". *Courtesy of Angela Pilgreen.* $35-45.

English style thatched cottage pottery set. $195-225 for the set.
Left. Sugar, 4.75".
Center front. Honey jar, salt shaker, and pepper shaker, 4.75".
Center rear. Platter with lid, 5.5".
Right. Creamer, 3.25".
The set is *Courtesy of Angela Pilgreen.*

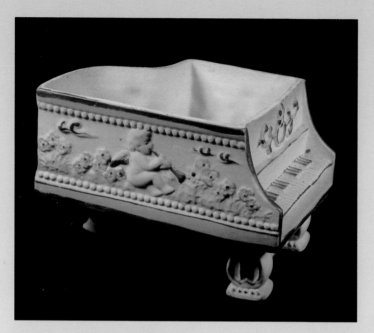

Bisque piano (lid is missing), 3" tall and 5" long. *Courtesy of Angela Pilgreen*. $15-20.

Another view of bisque piano.

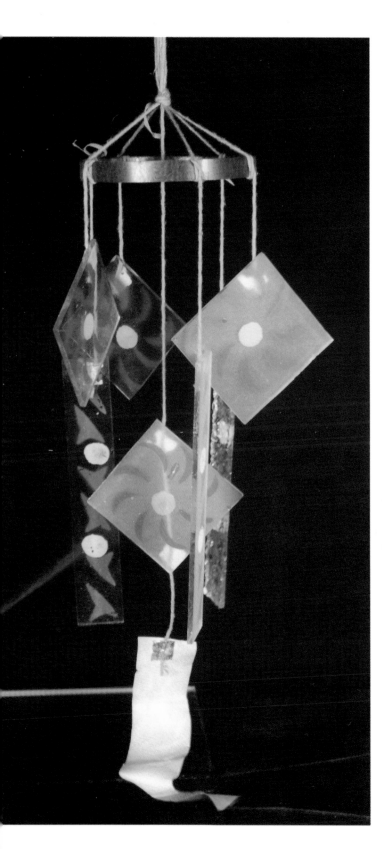

Wind chimes, 11"
at longest part.
*Courtesy of Angela
Pilgreen.* $20-30.

Left. Incense burner in shape of cottage, 5". $35-45.
Right. Incense burner in shape of man with sombrero, 4". $15-25.
The incense burners are *Courtesy of Angela Pilgreen*.

Strawberry cookie jar, 5". *Courtesy of Joyce Calhoun*. $45-55.

Four papier maché plates with fruit scene, 5.25" in diameter. Front plate contains paper umbrella. *Courtesy of Angela Pilgreen.* $15-18 each.

Two wooden bowls, 6" in diameter. *Courtesy of Angela Pilgreen.* $18-22 each.

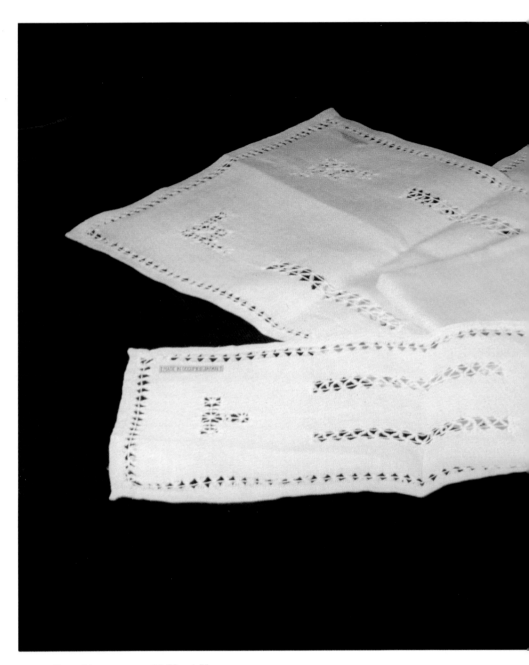

Front. Linen runner, 10.5" x 4.5".
Left and center rear. Linen mats, each is 12" x 8.25".
Right. Linen runner, 40" x 15". $45-55 for the set.
The linen items are *Courtesy of Angela Pilgreen.*

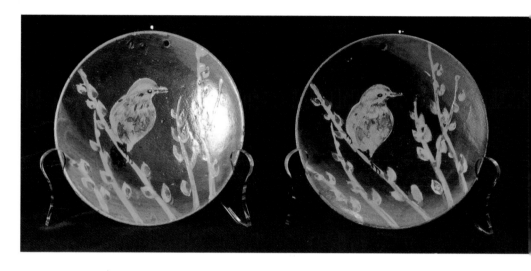

Two papier maché plates with design of bird, 4.25" in diameter. *Courtesy of Angela Pilgreen.* $15-18 each.

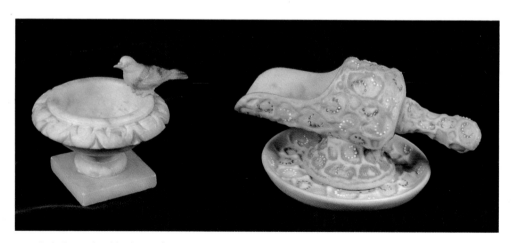

Left. Stone bird bath, 3". $35-45.
Right. Stone Ardalt scoop, 3". $45-55.
The items are *Courtesy of Angela Pilgreen.*

Left. Mother cup, 3.25". $18-22.
Center. Strawberry mustard jar, 3.5". $25-35.
Right. Teapot, measures 5". $25-35.
The items are *Courtesy of Angela Pilgreen*.

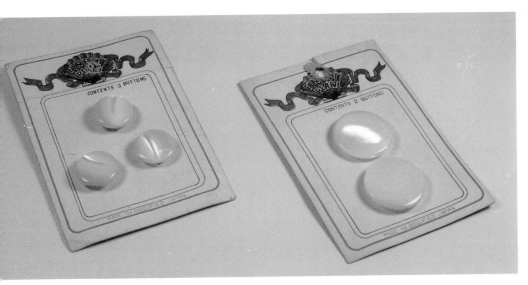

Two cards with pearl buttons, 3.5" x 2.25". *Courtesy of Mary G. Moon.* $6-8.

Silk scarf, 36" x 36". *Courtesy of Mary G. Moon.* $35-45.

Left. Toothpick holder with man wearing sombrero, 2.75". $15-18.
Center. Cup, 1.5". $9-12.
Right. Match holder with likeness of boy, 2.25". $25-35.
These items are *Courtesy of Angela Pilgreen*.

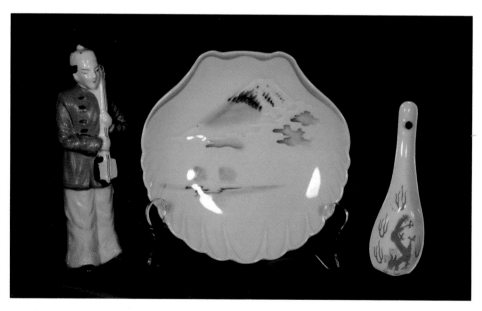

Left. Oriental man holding musical instrument. $25-35.
Center. Blue and white plate with mountain scene. $12-16.
Right. Spoon. $9-12.

Top. Bisque shelf boy, 3.25. $12-18
Bottom left. Old man, 5.25". $19-22.
Bottom center. Black man, 3.5". $20-30.
Bottom right. Old man (missing an arm), 5.25". $25-35.
Figurines are *Courtesy of Angela Pilgreen*.

Left. Telephone, 1.25" long. $8-12.
Front center. Celluloid "See no evil, speak no evil, hear no evil" figures, 0.75". $15-18.
Back center. Teapot, 2.5". $12-15.
Right. "See no evil, speak no evil, hear no evil" figures, 2.25" x 1.25". $10-12.
These items are *Courtesy of Angela Pilgreen.*

Left. Teapot. $12-16.
Right. Telephone. $9-12.
The items are *Courtesy of Karen Reavis.*

Left. Windmill for fish bowl, 3.75". $18-22.
Right. English style honey jar, 3.25". $35-45.
The items are *Courtesy of Karen Reavis*.

Left. Fish planter. $18-22.
Right. Vase with floral motif. $20-25.
The items are *Courtesy of Joyce Calhoun*.

Left. Humanoid girl, 2.75". $20-25.
Right. Humanoid boy, 2.5". $20-25.
The humanoids are *Courtesy of Angela Pilgreen*.

Left. Ice man humanoid, 4.5". $20-25.
Center left. Humanoid dressed as maid, 4.5". $20-25.
Center. Humanoid dressed as Indian chief, 4.5". $20-25.
Center right. Humanoid with flower on head, 4.5". $20-25.
Right. Humanoid, 4.5". $20-25.
The humanoids are *Courtesy of Ruth Derbin*.

Elves ashtray, 2.5".
Courtesy of Angela Pilgreen. $18-22.

159

Bibliography

Archambault, Florence. *Occupied Japan for Collectors*. Atglen,. Pennsylvania: Schiffer Publishing, Ltd., 1992.

Florence, Gene. *The Collectors Encyclopedia To Occupied Japan Collectibles. Third Series*. Paducah, Kentucky: Collector Books, 1987.

Florence, Gene. *The Collectors Encyclopedia To Occupied Japan Collectibles. Fourth Series*. Paducah, Kentucky: Collector Books, 1996.

Klamkin, Marian. *Made in Occupied Japan: A Collector's Guide*. New York: Crown Publishers, Inc., 1976.

Parmer, Lynette. *Collecting Occupied Japan with Values*. Atglen, Pennsylvania: Schiffer Publishing, Ltd., 1996.

Sieloff, Judie Ludwig. *Collectibles of Occupied Japan*. Des Moines, Iowa: Wallace-Homestead Book Co., 1978.